INVESTIGATING GHOSTS IN PRISONS

Matilda Snowden

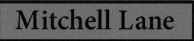

Mitchell Lane

PUBLISHERS

mitchelllane.com

2001 SW 31st Avenue
Hallandale, FL 33009

First Edition, 2021.
Author: Matilda Snowden
Designer: Ed Morgan
Editor: Joyce Markovics

Series: Investigating Ghosts!
Title: Investigating Ghosts in Prisons / by Matilda Snowden

Hallandale, FL : Mitchell Lane Publishers, [2021]

Library bound ISBN: 978-1-68020-637-1
eBook ISBN: 978-1-68020-638-8

CONTENTS

Words in **bold** can be found in the Glossary.

HAUNTED PRISONS

Rows of dark cells line a wide corridor in an old prison. The air is damp and chilly. Holding a digital recorder, a ghost hunter walks along the hallway, peering into the cells. The prisoners who once lived in them are long gone. But the ghost hunter feels something strange . . . as if she's being watched.

She continues to walk and record. Just then, what feels like an icy cold hand touches—and then grabs her. It tries to pull her into one of the cells. Stunned, she drops the recorder and **bolts** to the nearest exit.

Prisons are where thieves, kidnappers, murderers, and other criminals are locked up—sometimes for life. In the past, prisoners were often held in tiny, cramped cells like caged animals. Many became violent or went insane. Is this why so many old prisons are said to be haunted? Do spirits linger in places where many people suffered and died? There is a devoted group who want to find out. These ghost hunters, also known as paranormal investigators, gather evidence to prove that ghosts are real.

Turn the page to read frightening stories about reportedly haunted prisons. And follow teams of paranormal investigators who seek to uncover the truth about ghosts.

INTERESTING FACT

Prisons have gone by many names. In the past, they were sometimes called reformatories or penitentiaries. It was thought that criminals could be reformed, or changed, at reformatories. Penitentiary comes from the word *penitence*, which means "regret or remorse for having done wrong."

OHIO STATE REFORMATORY

Mansfield, Ohio

The Ohio State Reformatory looks more like a castle than a prison. The huge stone building contains 600 cells, spreading over six floors. It opened in 1896 and was soon filled to capacity. In the 1900s, the prison became very overcrowded. One story tells of two **inmates** who were forced to share a cell in **solitary confinement**. One of the prisoners went missing. His body was later found stuffed under the bed.

Countless others have died at the prison too, including Helen Glattke, a prison warden's wife. In 1950, when reaching for a box in her closet, Helen accidentally knocked over a loaded gun. As it fell to the floor, the gun fired, striking her in the chest. People say that when her spirit is present her favorite rose perfume fills the air.

INTERESTING FACT

Over the years, 154,000 inmates passed through Ohio State Reformatory's doors. The prison remained open for 94 years, closing in 1990. Today, the building is open to visitors.

The prison's dark and deadly past has attracted many paranormal investigators, including Jamie Davis. During a ghost hunt, Jamie and her partner Sam visited a waiting room in the old prison. Jamie carried a flashlight, which she sometimes uses to communicate with spirits. Then she noticed a strange gray mist. Soon after, she felt a presence. At that moment, the flashlight turned on by itself! Certain that a spirit was in the room, Jamie asked, "Can you let me know if you were a prisoner here?" The flashlight lit up again. All of a sudden, Jamie heard someone walking toward her. "Was that you making the noise? . . . Are you still here with me?" she asked. Once again, the flashlight turned on. Jamie asked the ghost to say its name into an audio recorder, hoping to capture an EVP. When she and Sam later listened to the recording, they heard what sounded like the name *Eugene Carter*.

INTERESTING FACT

EVP stands for "electronic voice phenomena." Ghost hunters believe that some audio devices can capture supernatural sounds or ghostly voices known as EVPs.

Jamie looked up the name *Eugene Carter* in the prison's database but didn't find a match. She was left wondering: Who was he? Had he died in the prison, and was his soul trapped there? The answers remain a mystery.

In 1932, prison guard Frank Hanger was beaten to death by Ohio State Reformatory inmates. It's said that his ghost haunts the prison. "We have had reports of [Hanger] . . . being spotted repeatedly, not only on camera but during a live investigation," says Molly Cabrera, a worker at the prison. One day, writer and ghost hunter Rami Ungar used a dowsing rod to try to contact Frank's spirit. In the area where Frank was killed, Rami asked, "Frank, are any of the people who caused your death also haunting this prison?" The rod quickly moved to an open "yes" position.

A man holds a dowsing rod, which is in the closed or "no" position.

Inside a room used by guards at the Ohio State Reformatory.

INTERESTING FACT

A dowsing rod is a metal y-shaped tool. Some people believe it's moved by unseen forces and can indicate yes or no answers. "Yes" is an open rod position, while "no" is a closed position. Paranormal investigators sometimes use it to communicate with spirits.

ALCATRAZ FEDERAL PENITENTIARY

San Francisco, California

Alcatraz sits on a rocky 22-acre island in San Francisco Bay. A shroud of fog often covers the prison. It housed some of the most menacing criminals on earth. Despite countless escape attempts, it's thought that no prisoner ever made it off "The Rock." Many were shot by guards or died in the cold, choppy waters of the bay. Their ghosts and others, it seems, are said to remain on the island.

Today, Alcatraz attracts over one million tourists each year. Witnesses have reported countless spooky experiences, including cell doors slamming on their own, ghostly whistling, and full-body apparitions. "It is an extremely haunted site," says paranormal investigator Mollie Stewart.

INTERESTING FACT

Long before it was a prison, local Native Americans collected birds' eggs on the island. Legend says that they never stayed long because they believed it was an evil place.

In 2003, ghost hunters Annette Martin, a psychic, and Loyd Auerbach went to Alcatraz. They entered an area called "the hole" where prisoners were locked up in solitary confinement. "I suddenly felt cold all over," said Annette, who remembers goose bumps on her skin. They walked into cell D-14. Loyd was carrying an EMF meter, which can pick up changes in electromagnetic fields. It suddenly went off. "I smell something dead," Annette then said. She and Loyd continued to cellblock C-104, where Annette saw blood all over the walls and heard moaning. "I have the sense that someone or several people have been murdered here!" said Annette. As it turns out, the cell was the sight of a bloody murder and escape attempt in 1946. Two guards and three inmates died.

The solitary confinement block, also known as "the hole."

BROADWAY

INTERESTING FACT

Ghost hunters believe that some spirits are made of energy. Therefore, tools like EMF meters can help them determine if a ghost is present. Paranormal investigators also use various digital recorders, thermal imaging tools, and other equipment to prove or disprove the existence of ghosts.

One of the most terrifying paranormal encounters happened to a prisoner in the 1940s. Soon after being thrown in "the hole," he screamed for help. The inmate described a creature with "glowing, red eyes" that was in the cell with him. The guards ignored him. The man yelled all night. In the morning, he was silent. When the guards opened the cell, they found his dead body. The prisoner had red marks on his neck as if he'd been strangled. Yet, according to the guards, no one had entered the man's cell. Even stranger, when the guards lined up all the inmates to count them, they claimed to see the dead man among them. Then, in a flash, he disappeared.

INTERESTING FACT

One of the most common scary sightings on Alcatraz is a Civil War soldier. A security guard named Eric had just finished up his overnight shift when he nearly fainted. Before his eyes stood a ghostly soldier in a Civil War uniform. Eric was pale and shaking when he told the other guards about seeing the ghost.

WEST VIRGINIA STATE PENITENTIARY

Moundsville, West Virginia

On May 7, 2004, paranormal investigator Polly Gear snapped a famous photo at West Virginia Penitentiary. It was the middle of a stormy night. Polly was walking in the prison's north hallway when she heard a noise. "I flipped on my light and saw a black form of a human shadow walking toward me," she said. "It looked at its arm (where my light was on it), then it looked at me." Polly was able to get a

clear picture of the shadow person. It looked like "black vibrating static—such as you would see on a TV," she said. "I felt it was just as curious about me as I was of it." Polly then checked to see if there were any people in the area. No one was around. Polly has no doubt about what she saw and captured on film that night. It was a real shadow person "one that I saw with my own eyes."

INTERESTING FACT

Polly Gear is a co-founder of Mountaineer Ghosts Paranormal Investigators. Paranormal investigators believe that shadow figures are spirits that appear as human-shaped shadows or dark silhouettes.

Soon after it opened in 1867, West Virginia State Penitentiary was described as "hell on earth." During its dark history, prisoners were stuffed into five-by-seven-foot cells and some were executed in the prison's electric chair, nicknamed "Old Sparky." It's thought that over 1,000 people died there. It's not surprising that ghostly inmates are said to roam the prison.

Visitors have reported seeing, hearing, and being touched by ghosts. Shadow figures are especially common. In 2015, members of the Living Dead Paranormal Society went to the prison. They caught a shadow person on video and recorded many EVPs. One of the most shocking EVPs was a phantom voice saying, "Do you want to join them in hell?"

INTERESTING FACT

In 2012, a family touring the prison also captured a video of a shadow figure. Are the shadow figures long-dead prisoners?

CHAPTER FIVE

Eastern State Penitentiary

Philadelphia, Pennsylvania

When Eastern State Penitentiary opened in 1829, people were in awe. The giant, star-shaped building had lots of modern features, including running water and central heating. However, life in the prison was far from humane. Prisoners were kept alone nearly all the time and couldn't talk. When taken from their cells, hoods were tied over the inmates' heads so they couldn't see. They were also tortured. Some prisoners were strapped to walls or chairs, thrown into underground pits, or put in the Iron Gag, a metal restraint that could rip out a

person's tongue. Many went insane. Over the years, the prison has become known for its supernatural activity. Paranormal investigators Jason Hawes and Grant Wilson toured the prison in 2004.

INTERESTING FACT

Eastern State Penitentiary closed in 1971. As many as 80,000 inmates were housed there over the years, including gangster Al Capone and bank robber Willie Sutton.

Al Capone

Jason, Grant, and their team set up cameras and recorders around the prison. One of their crew was taking a photo in cellblock 4 when he spotted a curious black shape. "It went right across my face. I saw shoulders and a head," he said. He was so startled that he ran from the cell.

The team also recorded a short, shadowy figure in a cloak in cellblock 12. They later went back to the cell to capture more footage of the cloaked man. Jason and Grant felt a heaviness in the room, and Grant was "having trouble moving his feet." Suddenly, they saw movement. A shadow slipped out of a cell and disappeared. After reviewing hours of footage and their up-close ghostly encounters, Jason and Grant concluded, "that the building was haunted." Are they correct? Only you can decide.

GHOST-HUNTING TOOLS

Here are some basic ghost-hunting tools. Many household items can be used to track and gather evidence of possible ghosts.

- Pen and paper to record your findings

- A flashlight with extra batteries

- A camera with a clean lens. Sometimes, the "**orbs**" that some people capture on film are actually dust particles on the lens.

- A cell phone to use in case of an emergency and to keep track of time

- A camcorder or digital video recorder to capture images of spirits or any other paranormal activity

- A digital audio recorder to capture ghostly sounds or EVPs

- A digital thermometer to pick up temperature changes

More experienced ghost hunters use thermal imaging tools to locate hot and cold spots, as well as special meters to pick up energy fields. These include EMF (electromagnetic field) and RF (radio frequency) meters.

FIND OUT MORE

BOOKS

Gardner Walsh, Liza. *Ghost Hunter's Handbook: Supernatural Explorations for Kids*. Lanham, Maryland: Down East Publishing, 2016.

Loh-Hagan, Virginia. *Odd Jobs: Ghost Hunter*. Ann Arbor, Michigan: Cherry Lake Publishing, 2016.

Rudolph, Jessica. *Deserted Prisons (Tiptoe Into Scary Places)*. New York: Bearport Publishing, 2017.

WEBSITES

American Hauntings
https://www.americanhauntingsink.com

American Paranormal Investigations
https://www.ap-investigations.com

The Atlantic Paranormal Society
http://the-atlantic-paranormal-society.com

Ghost Research Society
http://www.ghostresearch.org

Paranormal Inc.
http://www.paranormalincorporated.com

The Parapsychological Association
https://www.parapsych.org

WORKS CONSULTED

Auerbach, Loyd, and Annette Martin. *The Ghost Detectives' Guide to San Francisco*. Fresno California: Craven Streat Books, 2011.

Davis, Jamie. *Haunted Asylums, Prisons, and Sanatoriums*. Woodbury, Minnesota: Llewellyn Publications, 2013.

Hawes, Jason, and Grant Wilson. *Ghost Files*. New York: Gallery Books, 2011.

Newman, Rich. *Ghost Hunting for Beginners: Everything You Need to Know to Get Started*. Woodbury, Minnestota: Llewellyn Publications, 2018.

Person, Stephen. *Horrorscapes: Ghostly Alcatraz Island*. New York: Bearport Publishing, 2011.

Rule, Leslie. *When the Ghost Screams: True Stories of Victims Who Haunt*. Kansas City, Missouri: Andrews McMeel Publishing, 2006.

Taylor, Troy. *The Ghost Hunters Guidebook: The Essential Guide to Investigating Ghosts & Hauntings*. Alton, Illinois: Whitechapel Productions Press, 2004.

ON THE INTERNET

http://www.angelsghosts.com/moundsville_penitentiary_shadow_man_ghost_picture

https://beyondthesixthsense.wordpress.com/2015/09/15/shocking-footage-ghost-hunters-capture-spirit-shadow-on-camera/

https://www.easternstate.org/research/history-eastern-state

https://www.ghostsofohio.org/lore/ohio_lore_33.html

https://www.mrps.org/blog/2017/11/22/shocking-proof-of-10-real-life-ghost-stories-at-an-ohio-prison

https://www.mrps.org/learn/history/ghostly-history-of-osr

https://www.nps.gov/alca/learn/nature/index.htm

https://wvpentours.com/about/history/articles/the-greenbrier-ghost/

https://www.youtube.com/watch?v=PBzFIRFRfxk

GLOSSARY

apparition
A ghost or ghostlike image

awe
A feeling or respect mixed with fear or wonder

bolts
Runs or moves quickly

criminals
People who have done bad or unlawful things

devoted
Very loyal

electromagnetic fields
Fields of energy around a magnetic material or moving electric charges

evidence
Information and facts that help prove something

executed
Put to death

humane
Showing compassion or kindness

inmates
People confined to a prison

menacing
Dangerous or threatening

orbs
Glowing spheres

paranormal
Events not able to be scientifically explained

phantom
Belonging to a ghost or spirit

presence
A person or thing that exists but is not seen

psychic
A person who has powers beyond scientific explanation, such as telepathy or clairvoyance

restraint
Something that keeps someone under control

shroud
A thing that covers or obscures something

silhouettes
The dark shapes and outlines of someone or something

solitary confinement
The isolation of a prisoner in a separate cell as a punishment

spirits
Supernatural beings such as ghosts

supernatural
Beyond scientific understanding

thermal
Relating to heat

Index

About the Author

Matilda Snowden loves all things old and cobwebby and learning about historic prisons, especially Sing Sing Correctional Facility in Ossining, New York. Her favorite thing about being an author is talking with children about how to tell a spooky story.